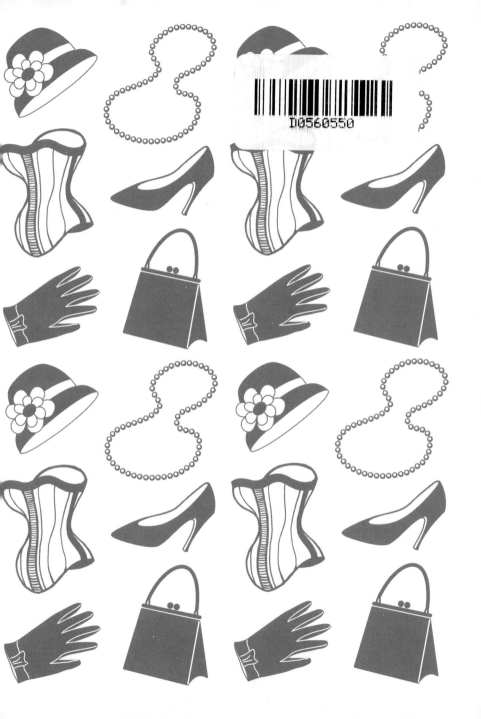

SOME LIKE IT HOT COOKBOOK

SARAH KEY
GAIL MONAGHAN

ABBEVILLE PRESS PUBLISHERS
New York London Paris

ALSO AVAILABLE IN THE HOLLYWOOD HOTPLATES™ SERIES

The Casablanca Cookbook ★ *A Christmas Carol Cookbook*
Gone with the Wind™ Cookbook ★ *The "I Love Lucy" Cookbook*
The Wizard of Oz™ Cookbook ★ *It's a Wonderful Life™ Cookbook*

DESIGNER: Patricia Fabricant
PRODUCTION EDITOR: Meredith Wolf
PICTURE EDITOR: Laura Straus
PRODUCTION MANAGER: Lou Bilka

First edition
2 4 6 8 10 9 7 5 3 1

Library of Congress Cataloging-in-Publication Data
Key, Sarah.
The Some like it hot cookbook / Sarah Key, Gail Monaghan.
p.   cm.
Includes index.
ISBN 0-7892-0244-1
1. Cookery, Cuban. 2. Menus. 3. Some like it hot (Motion picture) I. Monaghan, Gail. II. Title.
TX716.C9K49   1996
641.597291—dc20   96-2727

Metric Conversions: 1 teaspoon = 5 ml; 1 tablespoon = 14.8 ml.

CONTENTS

COCKTAIL PARTY IN UPPER SEVEN 5

DINNER WITH SWEET SUE
AND HER SOCIETY SYNCOPATORS 19

BARBECUE ON THE BEACH 27

DINNER AT THE CUBAN ROADHOUSE 35

MIDNIGHT SUPPER ON
THE YACHT 45

BIRTHDAY BANQUET
FOR SPATS 53

LIST OF RECIPES 64

COCKTAIL PARTY
IN UPPER SEVEN

OLGA: Here's the cocktail shaker.

GIRLS: Easy on the vermouth.
If we only had some ice—Pass the peanut butter.
Anybody for salami?

JERRY: Thirteen girls in a berth—that's bad luck!
Twelve of you will have to get out! . . . Please,
girls, *no more food!* I'll have *ants* in the morning!

GREASED LIGHTNING SMOKED SALMON CANAPÉS

SUGAR: You don't know what they're like. You fall for them and you love 'em—you think it's going to be the biggest thing since the Graf Zeppelin—and the next thing you know they're borrowing money from you and spending it on other dames and betting the horses—
JOE: You don't say?
SUGAR: Then one morning you wake up and the saxophone is gone and the guy is gone, and all that's left behind is a pair of old socks and a tube of toothpaste, all squeezed out.

30 slices (1 loaf) "very thin" white bread
4 teaspoons freshly squeezed lime juice
¼ teaspoon Dijon mustard
¾ cup (180 ml) olive oil
1 teaspoon finely minced garlic
1 tablespoon finely minced shallot
1 fresh chili pepper, seeds and ribs removed, finely minced
sea salt, freshly ground black pepper, and Tabasco to taste
1 pound (460 g) boiling potatoes, peeled and cut into ¼-inch (6.5-mm) dice
¾ pound (340 g) smoked salmon, thinly sliced, cut into ¼-inch (6.5-mm) squares
2 tablespoons finely minced fresh chives

To make toast rounds, preheat oven to 350° F (180° C). With 2-inch (5-cm) cookie cutter, cut 2 rounds from each bread slice. Do not use crust. Place rounds on baking sheet and bake 8 minutes; turn once and bake until both sides are dry and deep gold, 3 or 4 more minutes. Cool on wire rack.

To make dressing, whisk lime juice with mustard in small bowl. Slowly add olive oil and whisk until an emulsion forms. Stir in garlic, shallot, and chili pepper. Add salt, pepper, and Tabasco to taste. Set aside. Cook potatoes in boiling, salted water until just cooked, about 2 minutes. Do not overcook or potatoes will disintegrate in salad. Refresh in cold water, drain well, wrap in kitchen towel to dry, and set aside. In large bowl, toss salmon, potatoes, and chives with dressing. Cover and refrigerate for at least 3 hours. Serve at room temperature, dividing salmon mixture evenly among toast rounds.

MAKES APPROXIMATELY 60 CANAPÉS.

MINI GRILLED CHEEJE WITH JPICY JURPRIJE CENTERJ

SUGAR: What's the surprise?
JERRY: Uh-uh. Not yet.
SUGAR: When?
JERRY: We better have a drink first.
SUGAR: Here. This'll put hair on your chest.
JERRY: No fair guessing.

12 slices "very thin" white bread
six 3-inch (7.5-cm) squares presliced Jack or Muenster cheese
1½ tablespoons finely minced garlic
1½ tablespoons finely minced fresh cilantro
1½ tablespoons finely minced fresh chili peppers
3 to 4 tablespoons unsalted butter or as needed

Cut crusts from bread and cut each slice into a 3-inch (7.5-cm) square. Cut slice into 4 little squares, approximately 1½ × 1½ inches (4 × 4 cm) each. Quarter each cheese slice into 4 equal squares. In small bowl, mix together minced garlic, cilantro, and chili peppers. Make 24 sandwiches by placing slice of cheese and ½ teaspoon of the minced condiments between each 2 slices of bread. Melt 2 tablespoons of butter in large skillet over medium heat and cook sandwiches on both sides until golden, about 2 minutes per side. If necessary, make in batches, adding more butter as needed. Keep finished sandwiches warm in a 275° F (135° C) oven until all are cooked. Serve hot.

MAKES 24 MINI SANDWICHES.

BUTTERY CHILI SHORTBREAD

JERRY: How about that talent? This is like falling into a tub of butter.

JOE: Watch it, *Daphne!*

JERRY: When I was a kid, I used to have a dream—I was locked up in this pastry shop overnight—with all kinds of goodies around—jelly rolls and mocha eclairs and sponge cake and Boston cream pie and cherry tarts—

JOE: Listen, stupe—no butter and no pastry. We're on a diet!

1 1/2 cups (360 g) unsalted butter at room temperature
1 large clove garlic, pushed through a garlic press or peeled and finely minced
1/3 cup (80 g) sugar
3 cups (360 g) flour
1 1/2 teaspoons paprika
1 1/4 teaspoons chili powder
1/4 teaspoon cayenne pepper
1/4 teaspoon freshly ground black pepper
1 teaspoon sea salt
1 tablespoon ground cumin
1 tablespoon ground coriander
2 1/2 teaspoons ground anise seed
1/2 teaspoon powdered saffron or crushed saffron threads

In bowl of electric mixer or by hand with wooden spoon, cream butter, garlic, and sugar until light and fluffy, about 5 minutes. Sift together the flour and spices. Add dry ingredients to butter mixture and beat on low speed until blended, scraping down sides of bowl with rubber spatula as necessary, or mix by hand with wooden spoon. Divide dough in half. Roll each half 3/16-inch (5-mm) thick between 2 sheets of waxed paper. Leave dough between waxed paper and refrigerate, well wrapped, for at least 30 minutes or up to 3 days. When ready to bake, preheat oven to 350° F (180° C). Using 1- to 2-inch (2.5- to 5-cm) cookie cutter, cut rounds from dough and place on greased or parchment-lined baking sheets. Bake until lightly colored, about 15 minutes. If dough is too brittle to cut without cracking, let it sit a few minutes after removal from refrigerator before cutting. Cool on wire racks. Store in an airtight container for up to a week or at least 6 weeks in freezer.

MAKES 30 TO 60 ROUNDS.

FIGS IN DRAG

JERRY: Who are we kidding? Look at that—look how she moves—it's like Jell-O™ on springs—they must have some sort of a built-in motor. I tell you it's a whole different sex.

6 large fresh figs
6 thin slices of Serrano ham (or prosciutto)
about 3 tablespoons extra-virgin olive oil
freshly ground black pepper to taste
about 1 tablespoon freshly squeezed lime juice

Four hours or less before serving, cut figs and ham slices lengthwise into quarters, making 24 pieces of each. Roll each fig quarter tightly in length of ham and secure with toothpick. Using pastry brush, paint each wrapped fig lightly with olive oil and grind a bit of pepper over the top. Cover with plastic wrap and set aside. When ready to cook, prepare charcoal fire or preheat electric grill or broiler. Cook figs about a minute on each side. They should be warmed through and just beginning to color. Transfer figs to platter and remove toothpicks. Drizzle each with a little more olive oil and a few drops of lime juice. Pass figs with fresh toothpicks and cocktail napkins.

MAKES 24 PIECES.

PUT-OUT MINI PIZZAS

NELLIE: What a heel! I spend four dollars to get my hair marcelled, I buy me a new negligee, I bake him a great big pizza pie . . . and where were you?

16 ounces (460 g) puff pastry dough
1 1/2 tablespoons unsalted butter
1 1/2 tablespoons extra-virgin olive oil
2 pounds (920 g) yellow onions, peeled and thinly sliced
2 cloves garlic, peeled and finely minced
3 jalapeño peppers, seeds and ribs removed, finely minced
2 teaspoons fresh thyme or 1 teaspoon dried
1/2 teaspoon sugar
1 1/4 teaspoons sea salt or to taste
pepper to taste
about 20 cherry tomatoes or enough to make 40 very thin slices
20 anchovy fillets, cut in half lengthwise and then again crosswise, making 80 pieces

To make crust, roll puff pastry dough with rolling pin to 3/16-inch (5-mm) thickness. Using 3-inch (7.5-cm) cookie cutter, cut out as many rounds as possible. Reroll dough and cut out more rounds until all dough is used, about 40 rounds. Refrigerate or freeze on baking sheet for at least 30 minutes or up to 3 days before baking. In large sauté pan or casserole, melt butter with olive oil over low heat. Add sliced onions, garlic, jalapeños, thyme, sugar, salt, and pepper. Cook, stirring frequently, until onions are soft and liquid has evaporated, about 20 to 30 minutes. Taste for salt and pepper. This topping can be made up to 3 days ahead and refrigerated until ready to use.

Preheat oven to 350° F (180° C). Remove baking sheet with rounds from refrigerator or freezer. Spread thin layer of onion mixture on each, center tomato slice on top, and make cross on top of tomato using 2 pieces of anchovy fillet. Bake on center oven rack until pizzas are piping hot and crust is golden, about 25 to 30 minutes. Remove pizzas from oven. Serve hot, warm, or at room temperature. Pizzas may be made several hours ahead, but do not refrigerate.

MAKES 40 MINI PIZZAS.

CORSETLESS CREAM CHEESE SPREAD

ROSELLA: Take your corsets off and spread out.
JERRY: Oh, I never wear one.
OLGA: Don't you bulge?
JERRY: Oh, no. I have the most divine little seamstress that
comes in once a month—and my dear, she's so *inexpensive*.

6 ounces (180 g) cream cheese, at room temperature
2 teaspoons finely minced garlic or to taste
1 tablespoon peeled and finely minced shallot
1 tablespoon finely minced fresh cilantro
1 jalapeño pepper, seeds and ribs removed, finely minced
sea salt, freshly ground black pepper, and Tabasco to taste

Cream the cheese, garlic, shallot, cilantro, jalapeño, and seasonings in electric mixer
or by hand. Serve immediately or cover and refrigerate up to 3 days. Bring to room
temperature before serving. Serve with raw vegetables, crackers, or Buttery Chili
Shortbread (p. 8).

MAKES APPROXIMATELY 1/2 CUP (120 G).

CHILI-MARINATED CHEVRE

GIRLS: Here's the vermouth. I brought some crackers and cheese. Will ten cups be enough? Can you use a bottle of Southern Comfort?

one 11-ounce (320 g) log mild goat cheese (such as plain Montrachet)
1 cup (240 ml) best-quality extra-virgin olive oil
4 to 6 cloves garlic, peeled and smashed with side of large knife
1 shallot, peeled and thinly sliced
2 tablespoons finely minced fresh hot chili peppers of your choice
several small sprigs fresh thyme or 1 teaspoon dried thyme
¼ teaspoon freshly ground black pepper
Tabasco to taste
1 tablespoon red peppercorns, crushed, divided
2 tablespoons finely minced fresh cilantro

Using large sharp knife, cut cheese crosswise into 8 equal slices, dipping knife into hot water between each cut. In shallow dish just large enough to comfortably hold sliced cheese, mix olive oil with garlic, shallot, chili peppers, thyme, pepper, Tabasco, and 2 teaspoons of crushed red peppercorns. Place cheese slices, side by side, in flavored oil and turn them once so that both sides of each slice are well coated with oil. Cover and refrigerate at least 24 hours and up to 4 days. Turn cheese slices at least once a day, spooning some oil and herbs over top each time. When ready to serve, bring cheese to room temperature. Arrange slices on serving platter with oil and herbs. Cheese slices are easiest to move while still cold. Sprinkle remaining teaspoon red peppercorns and minced cilantro over tops. Pass cheese with a basket of toast rounds or crackers (toast rounds from p. 6 work well here).

MAKES 8 SLICES.

FUZZY MANGO DAIQUIRI

SUGAR: *All the girls drink—but I'm the one that gets caught. That's the story of my life. I always get the fuzzy end of the lollipop.*

1/4 cup (60 ml) white rum
1 tablespoon curaçao
1 tablespoon freshly squeezed lime juice
1 1/2 teaspoons superfine sugar
1/2 cup (80 g) peeled and chopped fresh ripe mango
3/4 cup (120 g) crushed ice
fresh mint sprig

Put all ingredients except mint into blender. Process until smooth. Pour into tall glass, garnish with mint, and serve.

MAKES 1 COCKTAIL.

PROHIBITION PIÑA COLADA

1/4 cup (60 ml) light rum (omit for delicious virgin colada)
2 tablespoons unsweetened pineapple juice
2 tablespoons freshly squeezed lime juice
2 tablespoons cream of coconut (such as Coco Lopez)
1/4 cup (40 g) finely chopped very ripe fresh pineapple or unsweetened canned pineapple
1 cup (160 g) crushed ice
maraschino cherry
pineapple slice

Place all ingredients except garnishes in blender. Process to combine, 20 to 30 seconds. Pour into tall glass, garnish with cherry and pineapple, and serve.

MAKES 1 COCKTAIL.

FRESHLY SQUEEZED
WHITE RUM PUNCH

JOE: So you got pinched in the elevator. So what?
Would you rather be picking lead out of your navel?

ice cubes
3 tablespoons white rum
2 tablespoons freshly squeezed lime juice
2 tablespoons freshly squeezed orange juice
2 tablespoons unsweetened pineapple juice
1 teaspoon grenadine
maraschino cherry
fresh mint sprig

Fill tall glass 3/4 full with ice cubes. Pour in rum, juices, and grenadine. Stir to combine. Garnish with cherry and mint and serve.

MAKES 1 COCKTAIL

CUBA LIBRE

GIRLS: Aw, don't be a flat tire. Have a Manhattan.
Come on in. There's lots of room in the back.

3 tablespoons light rum
3 ounces (90 ml) Coca-Cola
freshly squeezed juice of 1/2 lime
ice cubes
1 lime slice

Stir together rum, Coca-Cola, and lime juice in tall glass. Fill glass with ice cubes and garnish with lime.

MAKES 1 COCKTAIL.

BANANA REPUBLIC DAIQUIRI

JERRY: We're going to sell the bracelet, and grab a boat to South America and hide out in one of those banana republics. The way I figure is, if we eat nothing but bananas, we can live there for fifty years—maybe a hundred years—that is if we get out of the hotel alive.

1/4 cup (60 ml) white rum
1 tablespoon banana liqueur or Triple Sec
1 tablespoon freshly squeezed lime juice
1 1/2 teaspoons superfine sugar
1/2 cup (80 g) mashed or chopped very ripe banana
3/4 cup (120 g) crushed ice
fresh mint sprig

Put all ingredients except mint into blender. Process until smooth. Pour into a tall glass, garnish with mint, and serve.

MAKES 1 COCKTAIL.

MARY LOU'S MOJITO

MARY LOU: Party in Upper 7. Got a corkscrew?

2 tablespoons freshly squeezed lime juice
1 teaspoon superfine sugar
2 teaspoons finely minced fresh mint leaves
cracked ice
1/4 cup (60 ml) white rum
2 tablespoons club soda
1 lime slice

Stir together lime juice, sugar, and mint leaves in tall glass, until sugar dissolves. Fill glass 3/4 full with cracked ice. Add rum and club soda and stir again. Garnish with lime.

MAKES 1 COCKTAIL.

JOE & JERRY'S RUM RUNNER

JERRY: We got to get out of town. Maybe we ought to grow beards.
JOE: We *are* going out of town. But we're going to shave.
JERRY: Shave? At a time like this? Those guys got machine guns—
they're going to blast our heads off—and you want to shave?
JOE: Shave our *legs*, stupid.

2 tablespoons blackberry brandy
2 tablespoons banana liqueur
1 tablespoon grenadine
1 tablespoon 151 rum (or other high-proof white rum)
2 tablespoons dark rum
2 tablespoons freshly squeezed lime juice
3/4 cup crushed ice
1 lime slice

Place all ingredients except lime slice in blender. Blend until smooth. Pour into tall glass, garnish with lime, and serve.

MAKES 1 COCKTAIL.

MIAMI CROSS-DRESSER

JERRY: But Joe—three weeks in Florida!
We could borrow some clothes from the girls in the chorus—
JOE: You've flipped your wig!
JERRY: Now you're talking! We pick up a couple of second-hand wigs—
a little padding here and there—call ourselves Josephine and Geraldine.

1/4 cup (60 ml) dark rum (such as Meyer's)
2 tablespoons 151 rum (or other high-proof white rum)
1 1/2 tablespoons freshly squeezed lime juice
1 1/2 tablespoons freshly squeezed grapefruit juice

1/4 cup (60 ml) club soda
1 1/2 tablespoons superfine sugar
3 leaves fresh mint, crushed
1/8 teaspoon Angostura bitters or to taste
crushed ice
1 lime slice

Stir together all ingredients, except crushed ice and lime slice, in 16-ounce glass. Add enough crushed ice to fill glass, garnish with lime, and serve.

MAKES 1 COCKTAIL.

HONEYED GOOD NIGHT PUNCH

SUGAR: (sticking her head out) Good night, honey.
JERRY: (to Joe, enraptured) Honey—she called me honey. (Without a word, Joe takes the ladder leaning against Jerry's berth, slides it under the lower.)
JERRY: What are you doing?
JOE: I just want to make sure that *honey* stays in the hive.
There'll be no buzzing around tonight.

1 cup (160 g) crushed ice
1 1/2 ounces (45 ml) dark rum
3 tablespoons freshly squeezed orange juice
2 teaspoons freshly squeezed grapefruit juice
1/2 teaspoon honey
Angostura bitters to taste
freshly grated nutmeg
fresh mint sprig

Combine all ingredients except nutmeg and mint in cocktail shaker. Stir well to dissolve honey, then shake hard to cool and combine. Pour into tall glass, garnish with nutmeg and mint, and serve.

MAKES 1 COCKTAIL.

Dinner with Sweet Sue and Her Society Syncopators

SUE: That's it for tonight, folks. This is Sweet Sue, saying good night, and reminding all you daddies out there—every girl in my band is a virtuoso—and I intend to keep it that way!

CARIBBEAN CHICKEN FRICASSEE

MARINADE

4 cloves garlic, peeled and finely minced

1 medium onion, peeled and finely chopped

2 teaspoons curry powder

2 teaspoons dried thyme or several sprigs fresh thyme

2 tablespoons finely minced chives or scallions

2 to 3 tablespoons finely minced fresh marjoram or basil

2 tablespoons finely minced fresh parsley

1 Scotch bonnet or other small red hot chili pepper, seeds and ribs removed and finely minced, or $1/4$ teaspoon Tabasco

$1 1/2$ teaspoons sea salt

$1/2$ teaspoon freshly ground black pepper

freshly squeezed juice of 1 lemon

two 3- to $3 1/2$-pound (1.5- to 2-kg) chickens, cut into 8 pieces each

2 to 3 tablespoons sugar

3 ribs celery, thinly sliced

3 carrots, peeled and cut into thin rounds

1 large onion, peeled and diced

3 cups (480 g) fresh or canned tomatoes, chopped

4 cups (640 g) cooked white rice, kept warm

Stir together marinade ingredients in large bowl. Add chicken and toss to coat chicken pieces with marinade. Cover bowl and refrigerate at least 6 hours (24 hours is better and up to 2 days is fine). Stir occasionally. When ready to cook, bring chicken to room temperature. Remove chicken from marinade, scraping off remaining bits. Reserve marinade. Place large casserole over medium heat. When hot, add sugar and stir with wooden spoon until caramelized and deep brown. Do not let sugar burn. Add chicken and brown on both sides, again being careful to avoid burning. When chicken pieces are deep gold, transfer to platter. Add celery, carrots, onion, and reserved marinade to pan. Cook over low heat, scraping up browned bits from bottom of pan and stirring frequently until vegetables have softened and are lightly colored, 15 to 20 minutes. To prevent burning, add a few tablespoons of water if needed. When vegetables are soft, add tomatoes to pan and bring them to simmer. Add chicken and any juices that have accumulated on platter. Stir and cover tightly. Turn heat to very low, and simmer until chicken is meltingly tender and ready to fall off bone, 1 to 1$\frac{1}{2}$ hours. Before serving, skim off fat that has risen to surface. If you have time, remove chicken from sauce, cool sauce, and remove fat that rises to top. To serve, reheat chicken with sauce, covered, over low heat or in warm oven. Serve over rice on individual plates or from platter.

MAKES 6 TO 8 SERVINGS.

BULL FIDDLE FRIED BANANAS

BELLHOP: Which of you dolls is Daphne?
JOE: Bull fiddle.
BELLHOP: It's from Satchel Mouth at Table Seven. (He breaks off one flower, hands it to Joe.) This is from me to you, doll.

3 tablespoons unsalted butter
3 tablespoons unflavored vegetable oil
1 small onion, peeled and cut in half
6 large bananas, slightly underripe, peeled and sliced on diagonal into $\frac{1}{2}$-inch (13-mm) slices
salt and freshly ground pepper to taste
1 lime cut into 6 or 7 wedges

Place frying or sauté pan, large enough to hold bananas in 1 layer, over medium-high heat. When pan is hot, add butter, oil, and onion halves, cut sides down. Stir onion for about 2 minutes to flavor oil. When pan and oil are very hot, add banana slices. Cook on first side until golden brown and crispy. Turn and cook slices on other side. When both sides are cooked, transfer bananas to paper toweling and blot. Discard onion. If necessary, bananas can be kept at this point for up to 20 minutes in warm oven. When ready to serve, season bananas with salt and pepper and serve with 1 lime wedge per person.

MAKES 6 TO 7 SERVINGS.

CITRUS SHRIMP SALAD

DOLORES: This a private clambake, or can anybody join?

DRESSING
1 1/2 tablespoons sherry vinegar
freshly squeezed juice and finely grated zest of 1 1/2 limes
5 tablespoons orange juice concentrate, defrosted
3/4 cup (180 ml) extra-virgin olive oil
2 shallots, peeled and finely minced
2 cloves garlic, peeled and finely minced
1 tablespoon finely minced jalapeño or serrano chili pepper
1 1/2 teaspoons sea salt or to taste
freshly ground black pepper and Tabasco to taste

24 jumbo shrimp, cooked, peeled, and deveined
1 large or 2 small bulbs of fresh fennel
3 large navel oranges
2 large avocados
1/4 cup (20 g) finely minced fresh chives or parsley

Whisk dressing ingredients together in small bowl and allow flavors to combine for at least an hour before serving. Slice shrimp in half lengthwise and set aside. Trim fennel and quarter it vertically. Slice each quarter into thin vertical slices; set aside. With small knife, peel oranges, removing all white pith along with peel. Slice peeled oranges crosswise into 1/4-inch (6.5-mm) slices. Set aside. When ready to serve, divide shrimp, fennel, and orange slices attractively among 8 plates. Peel and pit avocados. Cut each lengthwise into 16 pieces and add 4 pieces to each of 8 plates. Give dressing a whisk, adjust seasonings if necessary, and drizzle over salads. Sprinkle with fresh herbs and serve.

MAKES 8 SERVINGS.

PINEAPPLE-PAPAYA
SAXOPHONE-PLAYING SALSA

SUGAR: You see, I have this *thing* about saxophone players.
JOE: Really?
SUGAR: Especially tenor sax. I don't know what it is, but they just curdle me. All they have to do is play eight bars of "Come to Me My Melancholy Baby"—and my spine turns to custard, and I get goose-pimply all over—and I come to them.

freshly squeezed juice and finely grated zest of 2 large limes
1 tablespoon brown sugar
2 cups (320 g) finely diced, peeled, and cored fresh pineapple
1 cup (160 g) finely diced, peeled, and seeded fresh papaya
2 cloves garlic, peeled and finely minced
1 shallot, peeled and finely minced
1 jalapeño pepper, seeds and ribs removed, finely minced
¼ cup (20 g) fresh mint leaves, finely julienned
sea salt, freshly ground pepper, and Tabasco to taste

In large bowl, toss together all ingredients. Allow flavors to combine at least an hour at room temperature or overnight in refrigerator. Bring to room temperature before serving.

MAKES APPROXIMATELY 3 CUPS (480 G).

★ HOT TRIVIA ★

*Who was director Billy Wilder's first choice
for Jerry (Jack Lemmon)?*
Frank Sinatra.

LEMMON MERINGUE PIE

1 Lemmon Pie Crust (p. 25) or any prebaked 10-inch (25-cm) pie crust

CITRUS CURD FILLING
9 egg yolks
1 cup (240 g) sugar
pinch sea salt
finely grated zest and juice of 3 large lemons
finely grated zest of 2 oranges
1 cup (240 ml) freshly squeezed orange juice
2 tablespoons heavy cream

MERINGUE
6 egg whites, at room temperature
pinch sea salt
1/4 teaspoon cream of tartar
1 teaspoon lemon juice
1 teaspoon vanilla extract
1 1/2 cups (360 g) sugar plus 1 tablespoon for sprinkling

Prepare Lemmon Pie Crust or bake crust of your choice. To make filling, whisk together yolks, sugar, and salt in metal bowl or top half of double boiler. Add zests, juices, and cream and cook over simmering water until mixture is very thick, stirring constantly with wooden spoon. Using rubber spatula, scrape curd into clean bowl and cover immediately with plastic wrap. Smooth plastic wrap right onto surface of hot curd to eliminate all air, ensuring no skin forms on top. When completely cool, scrape curd into cooled crust, smooth the top, wrap well, and freeze until needed, at least 1 hour and up to 4 weeks.

To make meringue and finish pie, preheat oven to 325° F (165° C). By hand with wire whisk or with electric mixer, whisk egg whites with salt until frothy. Add cream of tartar, lemon juice, and vanilla. If using electric mixer, gradually increase speed. Once mixture is white and opaque, gradually add sugar. Beat until stiff. Remove pie from freezer and unwrap. Spread meringue over citrus curd in attractive pattern of swirls. Use all of meringue. Sprinkle top with 1 tablespoon sugar. Bake pie in middle of preheated oven until peaks of meringue begin to color, about 15 minutes. Let pie sit at room temperature at least 2 hours and up to 5 hours before serving, ensuring pie is completely defrosted.

MAKES ONE 10-INCH (25-CM) PIE.

LEMMON PIE CRUST

3 3/4 cups (450 g) flour
1 1/3 cups (240 g) confectioners' sugar
1/8 teaspoon sea salt
1 cup (240 g) unsalted butter, at room temperature
1 whole egg plus 1 egg yolk
finely grated zest of 1 lemon
seeds scraped from 1 vanilla bean or 1 teaspoon vanilla extract

Sift together flour, sugar, and salt. Cream butter with electric mixer or by hand until light and fluffy. Add dry ingredients and continue to mix until just combined. In small bowl, beat egg with egg yolk, lemon zest, and vanilla seeds or extract. Add this mixture to creamed ingredients and mix until combined. Form dough into ball and beat with rolling pin to flatten to thickness of 1 inch (2.5 cm) or thinner. Wrap the dough in plastic wrap and refrigerate for at least 30 minutes or up to 2 days. When ready to bake crust, preheat oven to 350° F (180° C). Roll dough into circle at least 15 inches (37.5 cm) across and about 3/16-inch (5-mm) thick. If dough is too cold, you may have to let it soften a few minutes before rolling. Butter pie pan 10 inches (25 cm) in diameter and 2 inches (5 cm) high (flan ring with removable bottom is preferred). Gently fit crust into pan. Prick bottom well with fork. If possible, refrigerate or freeze raw shell for at least 30 minutes at this point, so dough shrinks less. Line unbaked pastry with aluminum foil and fill with dried beans or pie weights. Bake pie shell in lower third of preheated oven about 15 minutes or until dough is just set. (It will no longer be shiny and will begin to look dry.) Remove weights and foil, reduce oven temperature to 300° F (150° C), and continue to bake until crust is deep gold, about 15 to 20 minutes more. Remove from oven and cool on wire rack.

MAKES ONE 10-INCH (25-CM) PIE CRUST.

BARBECUE ON THE BEACH

JOE: I got a funny sensation in my toes—
like somebody was barbecuing them over
a slow flame.

SUGAR: Let's throw another log on the fire.

SANDWICH OF MARINATED TUNA, PEPPERS, AND ONIONS

SUGAR: What a beautiful fish. . . What is it?
JOE: Oh—a member of the herring family.
SUGAR: Isn't it amazing how they get those big fish into those little glass jars?
JOE: They shrink when they're marinated.

MARINADE
1⅓ cups (320 ml) extra-virgin olive oil
6 tablespoons freshly squeezed lime juice
1½ teaspoons sea salt
½ teaspoon freshly ground black pepper
6 cloves garlic, peeled and minced
1 large shallot, peeled and minced
1 jalapeño pepper, seeds and ribs removed, finely minced
2 teaspoons grated fresh ginger
½ cup (40 g) chopped fresh parsley or cilantro
several sprigs fresh thyme or 1 teaspoon dried thyme

3 pounds (1.5 kg) best-quality tuna, cut into 1-inch (2.5-cm) steaks
2 large Spanish onions, peeled and cut crosswise into ¼-inch (6.5-mm) slices
2 red bell peppers, seeds and ribs removed, sliced vertically into eighths
2 green peppers, seeds and ribs removed, sliced vertically into eighths
sea salt and freshly ground pepper to taste
1 loaf Cuban Bread (p. 30) or 1 large loaf French bread
about 1½ cups Salsa Verde (p. 29)

Stir together marinade ingredients and let flavors combine, at least several hours or overnight if possible. Place fish and half of marinade in flat-bottomed dish or casserole just large enough to hold steaks side by side. Turn fish pieces over a few times to distribute marinade evenly. Spread onions and peppers evenly over fish, more or less in single layer, and spoon remaining marinade over top. Cover with plastic wrap, refrigerate, and allow to marinate 6 to 12 hours. Marinating process works best at room temperature, and unless kitchen is quite warm, fish can be kept unrefrigerated at least 4 hours of this time. Bring to room temperature before cooking. To cook tuna and vegetables, lightly oil and preheat electric grill or prepare fire for grilling over charcoal. When grill is ready, salt and pepper fish and vegetables and place over heat. Cook 3 minutes and then turn and cook other side. After 3 more minutes, check for doneness. If fish is not done, cook 1 or 2 minutes more. Tuna is best served rare or medium rare. It will continue to cook a bit off heat, so be careful. Cook vegetables until tender and a bit charred. Slice enough bread for 8 sandwiches. Spread each piece generously with Salsa Verde and then divide tuna slices and vegetables evenly among designated sandwich bottoms. Add the tops, press down gently to compress, and enjoy.

MAKES 8 SANDWICHES.

SALSA VERDE

2 cloves peeled garlic
1 shallot, peeled and quartered
1/2 teaspoon sea salt or to taste
1 1/2 tablespoons Dijon or Creole mustard
2 cups (160 g) watercress, leaves and tender stems, coarsely chopped
1 cup (80 g) fresh parsley, leaves and tender stems, coarsely chopped
1 cup (80 g) fresh cilantro, leaves and tender stems, coarsely chopped
3 tablespoons freshly squeezed lime juice
green (or red) Tabasco to taste
1/2 cup (120 ml) extra-virgin olive oil

In food processor, process garlic, shallot, salt, and mustard until fairly smooth paste is formed. Add greens, lime juice, and Tabasco and pulse until combined but with some texture remaining. You may need to stop machine and push greens down with rubber scraper once or twice. With machine running, add oil in steady stream until emulsion is formed. Pulse once or twice and scrape sauce into storage jar. Place plastic wrap directly on surface of sauce to eliminate all air and then cover with lid. Refrigerated this way, sauce should keep for up to 1 week.

NOTE: Sauce can be made with all watercress, all parsley, all cilantro, or proportioned as desired. Just be sure that greens are very fresh and total about 4 cups.

MAKES APPROXIMATELY 2 CUPS (480 G).

CUBAN BREAD

2 packages active dry yeast
1 tablespoon sugar
2 cups (480 ml) warm water (100 to 115° F/38 to 46° C)
1 tablespoon sea salt
5¹/₂ to 6 cups (660 to 720 g) all-purpose flour, divided
cornmeal for dusting

In large bowl, whisk together yeast, sugar, and warm water. Let mixture stand 5 to 10 minutes to proof before proceeding. Whisk in salt. Add 4 cups (480 g) flour, 1 cup (120 g) at a time, mixing with wooden spoon. Alternately, use electric mixer fitted with a dough hook attachment. Add remaining flour ¹/₂ cup (60 g) at a time, incorporating each addition before adding next. Stop adding flour when dough is no longer sticky. If kneading bread by hand, dust work surface with flour and knead dough approximately 8 to 10 minutes. If using electric mixer, knead about 5 minutes. In either case, add flour if dough becomes sticky while kneading, and knead until dough is smooth and elastic. Grease large bowl with butter or olive oil. Form dough into smooth ball. Roll around in bowl to grease it all over. Place it in bowl and cover tightly with plastic wrap. Allow dough to rise in warm place 1 to 2 hours until well doubled in size. Punch down dough and shape it again into smooth ball. Generously sprinkle baking sheet with cornmeal or line with parchment. Place dough in middle of sheet and press to flatten a bit. With razor or sharp knife, slash 2-inch (5-cm) grid on top and place in lower third of cold oven. Put pan of very hot water on oven floor or lowest rack just below bread. Shut oven and turn temperature to 400° F (200° C). Bake bread about 1 hour or until deep gold and it emits hollow sound when rapped on undercrust. After 30 minutes, remove pan of water. Completely cool bread on wire rack before slicing.

MAKES 1 LARGE LOAF.

SHELL OIL'S SLICED ISLAND SALAD

SUGAR: Oh, I'm not going to let *this* one get away. He's so cute—collects shells.

JOE: Shells? Whatever for?

JERRY: You know—the old shell game.

2 large flavorful tomatoes, cut crosswise into ½-inch (13-mm) slices

1 large red onion, peeled and thinly sliced

2 large avocados, peeled and pits removed, sliced into ½-inch (13-mm) wedges

2 red or yellow bell peppers, seeds and ribs removed,
cut into ¼-inch (6.5-mm) slices or rings

1 orange, cut crosswise into ⅛-inch (3-mm) slices

1 tablespoon freshly squeezed lime juice

1 teaspoon finely grated lime zest

½ teaspoon fresh ginger juice
(press about 1½ teaspoons grated fresh ginger root in garlic press)

3 tablespoons olive oil

sea salt and freshly ground pepper

¼ cup (20 g) finely chopped fresh parsley or cilantro or mixture of both

Arrange tomato, red onion, avocados, bell peppers, and orange slices attractively on platter. Whisk together lime juice, zest, ginger juice, and olive oil and drizzle over salad. Sprinkle with salt and pepper to taste and garnish with chopped herbs.

MAKES 6 TO 8 SERVINGS.

★ HOT TRIVIA ★

Why was Some Like It Hot *filmed in black and white?*
A test shot proved that the makeup for Tony Curtis and Jack Lemmon in drag was garish and unconvincing in color, so much to Marilyn Monroe's disappointment, the film was done in black and white.

SHORTBREAD DOUBLY ENDOWED WITH GINGER

SUGAR: But there's one thing I envy you for.
JERRY: What's that?
SUGAR: You're so flat-chested. Clothes hang so much
better on you than they do on me.

1½ cups (360 g) unsalted butter, at room temperature
¾ cup (180 g) sugar
1 egg, at room temperature
½ teaspoon vanilla extract
3¼ cups (390 g) flour
½ teaspoon sea salt
5 teaspoons powdered ginger
1½ cups (180 g) finely chopped crystallized ginger

In bowl of electric mixer or by hand with wooden spoon, cream butter and sugar until light and fluffy, 5 to 10 minutes. Add egg and vanilla and continue to beat another 3 to 5 minutes. Sift together flour, salt, and powdered ginger and add to batter. Beat just until blended. Stir in crystallized ginger. Divide dough in half and form into 2 balls. Flatten each ball between 2 pieces of waxed paper and roll with rolling pin to ³⁄₁₆-inch (5-mm) thickness. Refrigerate dough in its waxed paper on cookie sheets at least 30 minutes and up to 3 days (dough can also be frozen at this point for at least a month). When ready to bake cookies, preheat oven to 350° F (180° C). Use cookie cutters to cut rolled dough into shapes. Place raw cookies on greased or parchment-lined baking sheets and bake in preheated oven until cookies begin to color and are golden around the edges, 15 to 20 minutes depending on cookie size. Cool cookies on wire racks. When completely cool, store cookies in airtight container, where they will keep at least 1 week. They can also be frozen, well wrapped, for 1 month or more.

MAKES APPROXIMATELY 75 2-INCH (5-CM) ROUND COOKIES.

BROWN SUGAR RUM
ICE CREAM

JERRY: Boy, would I like to borrow a cup of that Sugar.
JOE: Look—no butter, no pastry, and *no Sugar!*

2 cups (480 ml) whole milk
2 cups (480 ml) heavy cream
1/2 cup (80 g) dark brown sugar
4 vanilla beans
6 egg yolks
2 to 4 tablespoons dark rum to taste

Put milk, cream, and brown sugar in medium heavy-bottomed saucepan. Slice vanilla beans lengthwise and scrape seeds from pods. Add seeds and pods to saucepan. Heat mixture until about to simmer. Turn off heat, cover pot, and steep at least 30 minutes. Whisk egg yolks in medium bowl. Reheat milk to simmer and add in slow steady stream to yolks while whisking constantly. Do not stop whisking, and do not add hot liquid too quickly or heat will curdle yolks. Return mixture to saucepan and place over low heat. Cook, stirring constantly with wooden spoon, until mixture begins to thicken. Do not let it come near boiling. If you feel safer using a deep-fry or candy thermometer, cook to 170° F (80° C). When ready, strain cream immediately into chilled bowl and cool to room temperature. Cover and refrigerate, at least 4 hours or overnight. Freeze in ice cream freezer according to manufacturer's directions. Just before ice cream is ready, add rum to taste. Churn another 1 or 2 minutes, transfer ice cream from machine to covered freezer jars, and freeze. Let ice cream soften slightly before serving.

MAKES APPROXIMATELY 1 1/2 QUARTS (1 1/2 LITERS).

DINNER AT THE CUBAN ROADHOUSE

JERRY: About that roadhouse—

OSGOOD: They've got a Cuban band that's the berries. Why don't we go there, blindfold the orchestra, and tango till dawn?

SUCCULENT CROWN ROAST OF PORK

OSGOOD: I am Osgood Fielding the Third.
JERRY: I am Cinderella the Second.
OSGOOD: If there's one thing I admire, it's a girl with a shapely ankle.
JERRY: Me too. Bye now.

MARINADE
freshly squeezed juice and finely grated zest of 2 limes
freshly squeezed juice and finely grated zest of 2 oranges
3 tablespoons dry sherry
12 cloves garlic, peeled and minced
2 bay leaves, crumbled
1 medium onion, peeled and chopped
2 teaspoons ground cumin, toasted
several drops Tabasco

1 crown roast of pork, 7 to 8 pounds (3.2 to 3.7 kg)
sea salt and freshly ground black pepper to taste

At least 6 hours before marinating meat, whisk together marinade ingredients. At least 24 hours before roasting, rub meat all over with marinade. Use it all, pouring extra over top. Cover roast and refrigerate. Turn meat several times while marinating. Remove roast from refrigerator 4 hours before cooking. When ready to cook, preheat oven to 425° F (215° C). Pat meat dry with paper towels and sprinkle liberally with salt and pepper. Place it upside down, resting on ends of rib bones, in shallow roasting pan. Reserve marinade. Put roast in oven and immediately reduce heat to 325° F (165° C). Pour ½ cup (120 ml) water into bottom of pan and baste frequently by spooning reserved marinade over meat. Cook meat about 1½ to 2 hours until meat thermometer registers 150° F (65° C). If pan dries out during cooking, add more water, sherry, or orange juice by ½ cup (120 ml). Do not let pan juices burn. When meat is done, transfer to platter and allow to rest for 10 minutes before slicing. During this time deglaze pan by adding 1 cup (240 ml) or so of water to pan juices. Simmer liquid on top of stove, scraping up anything stuck to bottom of pan. Taste for seasoning. Strain juices into sauceboat. When ready to serve, spoon off any fat that has risen to surface and adjust seasonings. Turn crown right-side up and place on platter. Serve with pan juices in sauceboat.

MAKES 16 RIB CHOPS, SERVING 8 TO 10.

MIXED-UP MANGO SALSA

JERRY: Osgood proposed to me. We're planning a June wedding.
JOE: What are you talking about? You can't marry Osgood.
JERRY: You think he's too old for me?
JOE: Jerry! You *can't* be serious!
JERRY: Why not? He keeps marrying girls all the time!
JOE: But you're not a girl. You're a guy! And why would a guy want to marry a guy?
JERRY: Security.

1/2 cup (60 g) red onion, peeled and finely minced
1 fresh, hot red chili pepper, seeds and ribs removed, finely minced
1 green chili pepper, seeds and ribs removed, finely minced
4 to 5 cups (640 to 800 g) peeled and diced ripe mango
(about 4 medium mangoes)
1/2 cup (40 g) fresh mint leaves, finely julienned
freshly squeezed juice and finely grated zest of 1 lime
4 teaspoons unflavored vegetable oil
1/2 teaspoon dark sesame oil
1/4 teaspoon sea salt or to taste
freshly ground pepper and Tabasco to taste

Toss together all ingredients in mixing bowl. Taste and adjust seasoning. Allow flavors to combine at least an hour before serving.

MAKES APPROXIMATELY 5 CUPS (800 G).

BIENSTOCK'S
BLACK BEAN SALSA

SUE: There are two things I will not put up with during working hours.
One is liquor—and the *other* one is men.
JERRY: We wouldn't be caught *dead* with men. Those rough, hairy
beasts with eight hands. They all want just one thing from a girl.
BIENSTOCK: I beg your pardon.

3 cups (480 g) cooked black beans or best-quality
canned black beans, well rinsed and drained
4 cloves garlic, peeled and finely minced
3/4 cup (90 g) finely diced red onion
2 canned chipotle chilis in adobo, finely minced
2 red bell peppers, roasted, peeled, seeded, and finely diced
1 ripe tomato, diced
1/4 cup (20 g) finely minced fresh cilantro or parsley
1/4 cup (20 g) thinly sliced scallion tops
2 teaspoons ground cumin, toasted
1 teaspoon chili powder
3 tablespoons freshly squeezed lime juice
2 tablespoons extra-virgin olive oil
1/2 teaspoon sea salt or to taste
Tabasco and freshly ground black pepper to taste

Toss together all ingredients in medium mixing bowl. Taste and adjust seasoning. Allow
flavors to combine for at least 1 hour. Adjust seasonings again just before serving.

NOTE: Fresh chilis and raw red bell peppers can be substituted for chilis in adobo
and roasted peppers in this recipe.

MAKES APPROXIMATELY 4 CUPS (640 G).

GARLIC-WILTED SPINACH

6 tablespoons extra-virgin olive oil
8 cloves garlic or more to taste, peeled and crushed
1/4 teaspoon red pepper flakes or to taste
4 to 5 pounds (1.8 to 2.3 kg) fresh young spinach leaves,
washed well and with stems removed
sea salt and freshly ground pepper to taste

Heat oil with garlic in large casserole over medium heat. Add red pepper flakes
and cook, stirring, for 1 or 2 minutes to flavor oil. Add as much spinach as will fit
in casserole. Using 2 wooden spoons, toss with hot oil. As it wilts, continue to add
spinach and toss until all spinach is in pot. Continue to cook and toss spinach until
just tender, 2 or 3 minutes more. Season with salt and pepper. Serve spinach hot,
lukewarm, or at room temperature.

MAKES 8 SERVINGS.

JERRY: Look, stop treating me like a child.
I'm not stupid. I know there's a problem.
JOE: I'll say there is!
JERRY: His mother—we need her approval.
But I'm not worried—because I don't smoke.
JOE: Jerry, there's *another* problem.
JERRY: Like what?
JOE: Like what are you going to do on your honeymoon?
JERRY: We've been discussing that. He wants to go to the Riviera,
but I sort of lean toward Niagara Falls.

RICH SWEET POTATOES
WITH A KICK

OSGOOD: You know, I've always been fascinated by show business.

JERRY: You don't say.

OSGOOD: Yes, indeed. It's cost my family quite a bit of money.

JERRY: You invest in shows?

OSGOOD: No—in showgirls. I've been married seven or eight times.

1½ cups (360 ml) heavy cream
3 jalapeño peppers, seeds and ribs removed, finely minced
6 cloves garlic, peeled and finely minced
¾ cup (90 g) finely minced onion
3 teaspoons finely grated orange zest
½ teaspoon sea salt or more to taste
Tabasco to taste
4½ cups (1080 g) mashed, cooked sweet potatoes or yams
(12 to 15 medium potatoes, baked)

Place cream, jalapeños, garlic, onion, zest, salt, and Tabasco in medium saucepan. Bring to boil over high heat. Boil, stirring often, until cream is reduced by half. Stir cream mixture into potatoes. Adjust seasoning and serve immediately, or refrigerate up to 2 days and reheat with a little milk or cream over low heat.

MAKES 10 SERVINGS.

CURRIED CORN MUFFINS

3/4 cup (90 g) yellow cornmeal
3/4 cup (90 g) all-purpose flour
2 tablespoons sugar
2 teaspoons baking powder
1 teaspoon salt
1/2 teaspoon ground cumin
1/2 teaspoon ground coriander
1 teaspoon curry powder
1/8 teaspoon cayenne pepper
1/4 teaspoon chili powder
5 tablespoons unsalted butter
2 fresh chili peppers, seeds and ribs removed, finely minced
2 cloves garlic, peeled and finely minced
1/2 cup (60 g) minced green or red bell pepper
1/2 cup (60 g) minced onion
1/2 cup (80 g) frozen corn kernels, defrosted, or fresh corn kernels cut off cob
1 1/2 cups (360 ml) milk
1 egg

Preheat oven to 425° F (215° C). Sift together cornmeal, flour, sugar, baking powder, salt, and spices and set aside. In medium skillet, melt butter and sauté chili peppers, garlic, bell pepper, and onion until vegetables are soft. Off heat, stir in corn kernels. Set aside to cool to lukewarm. In small bowl, whisk together milk and egg. Stir in cooled vegetables. Add this mixture to dry ingredients and stir to combine. Divide batter among 12-cup muffin tin lined with papers or nonstick muffin tin and bake until tops are deep gold, about 20 minutes. Serve hot.

MAKES 12 MUFFINS.

CARAMELZOWIED PINEAPPLE

OSGOOD: My last wife was an acrobatic dancer—
you know, sort of a contortionist. She could smoke a cigarette while
holding it between her toes—Zowie!—but Mama broke it up.
JERRY: Why?
OSGOOD: She doesn't approve of girls who smoke.

1 ripe pineapple
½ cup (120 g) unsalted butter
1 vanilla bean, split and seeds scraped off with a knife
1½ tablespoons freshly squeezed lime juice
½ cup (80 g) packed dark brown sugar
3 tablespoons dark rum
1 recipe Zesty Shortcake (p. 43), optional
*softened Brown Sugar Rum Ice Cream (p. 33) or sweetened whipped cream,
flavored with a few drops of vanilla extract*

Slice off bottom and top of pineapple and then rind. Cut peeled pineapple
lengthwise into eighths. Remove core sections and then cut each piece into ½-inch
(13-mm) slices. In sauté pan or skillet large enough to hold pineapple in single layer,
melt butter over medium heat. Add vanilla seeds and pod. When butter is bubbling,
add pineapple and lime juice. Sprinkle with brown sugar and cook, stirring, until
sugar is very dark and has begun to caramelize, with almost no liquid left. Warm
rum in small saucepan. Light rum with match or from gas burner by tipping pan just
enough for rum to ignite. *Off heat* pour flaming rum over pineapple, stirring and
shaking pan until flames have gone out. Remove vanilla pod from pan. When ready
to serve, place pan over low heat and gently rewarm contents, stirring. If serving
on shortcakes, split cakes horizontally. Spoon pineapple and sauce over cakes or
simply divide among 6 plates. Top with large spoonful of ice cream or sweetened
whipped cream or both. Add cake tops and serve.

MAKES 6 DESSERTS.

ZESTY SHORTCAKE

2 1/4 cups (270 g) all-purpose flour
1/3 cup (80 g) sugar
1 tablespoon baking powder
1/2 teaspoon sea salt
finely grated zest of 1 lime
1 cup (240 ml) heavy cream
1/2 teaspoon vanilla extract
about 2 tablespoons melted butter
about 3 tablespoons granulated sugar

Preheat oven to 350° F (180° C). Sift flour, sugar, baking powder, and salt into medium bowl. Stir in lime zest. Stir together cream and vanilla in electric mixer. Pour dry ingredients on top and mix briefly on low speed until almost combined. This can also be done by hand with a fork. Turn dough out onto floured board. Pat into ball, flatten, and roll to 1-inch (2.5-cm) thickness. Using 3-inch (7.5-cm) cutter, cut out 6 circles. Dough can be rerolled if necessary. Place shortcakes at least 1 inch (2.5 cm) apart on greased or parchment-lined baking sheet. Paint tops with melted butter and sprinkle lightly with sugar. Bake in center of preheated oven until light gold, about 25 minutes. Transfer cakes to wire rack. Serve warm or at room temperature.

MAKES 6 TO 8 SHORTCAKES.

JERRY: You know something, Mr. Fielding? You're dynamite!
OSGOOD: You're a pretty hot little firecracker yourself.

MIDNIGHT SUPPER ON THE YACHT

JOE: They run up a red-and-white flag on the yacht when it's time for cocktails.

SUGAR: You have a yacht? Which one is yours—the big one?

JOE: Certainly not. With all that unrest in the world, I don't think anybody should have a yacht that sleeps more than twelve.

NEW CALEDONIA
CURRIED CHICKEN

OSGOOD: *The New Caledonia.* That's the name of it. *The* Old *Caledonia* went
down during a wild party off Cape Hatteras. But tell her not to worry—
this is going to be a quiet little midnight snack—just the two of us.

JOE: Just the two of you? What about the crew?

OSGOOD: Oh, that's all taken care of. I'm giving them shore leave. We'll have a
little cold pheasant—and champagne—and I checked with the Coast Guard—there'll
be a full moon tonight—oh, and tell her I got a new batch of Rudy Valee records.

3 tablespoons unflavored vegetable oil, divided
1 large shallot, peeled and minced
2 garlic cloves, peeled and minced
1 teaspoon finely grated fresh ginger
1 tablespoon curry powder (preferably madras)
1/2 teaspoon ground cumin
1/8 teaspoon ground cinnamon
1/8 teaspoon chili powder
1 tablespoon mild honey or brown sugar
1 teaspoon dark sesame oil
*4 large chicken breasts, halved, boned, skinned, and pounded flat
into 8 paillards (butcher can do this)*
sea salt and freshly ground pepper to taste
1/2 cup (120 g) plus 2 tablespoons mayonnaise
freshly squeezed juice of 1/2 lime
freshly squeezed juice and finely grated zest of 1/2 orange
1 1/2 cups (180 g) bulb fennel or celery, trimmed and finely diced
1 cup (170 g) raisins plumped in hot water 30 minutes, drained
3 tablespoons minced fresh chives
few drops Tabasco

OPTIONAL GARNISHES

(use all, some, or none according to taste)
1/4 cup (40 g) each fresh papaya, avocado, and/or tomato, finely diced
fresh cilantro or parsley sprigs
3 tablespoons chopped, toasted peanuts
1/4 cup (20 g) grated fresh coconut (or shredded dried coconut)

Place small skillet over low heat. Add 1 tablespoon vegetable oil and shallots. Cook over low heat until translucent, about 10 minutes. Stir frequently and add bit of water occasionally if needed to prevent browning. Add garlic and ginger and cook 2 minutes more. Add curry, cumin, cinnamon, chili powder, and honey or sugar. Cook 3 minutes, adding a few tablespoons of water if mixture is very thick. Off heat, stir in sesame oil. Transfer mixture to large bowl to cool. Meanwhile season chicken with sea salt and pepper. Heat remaining 2 tablespoons vegetable oil in large skillet or sauté pan. Add paillards and brown on both sides over high heat, 1 to 2 minutes per side. Turn down heat and continue cooking until done, about 2 more minutes. Set aside to cool. When spice mixture is cool, stir in mayonnaise, lime juice, orange juice, and zest. Add fennel or celery, drained raisins, and chives. Add salt and pepper and Tabasco to taste. When chicken is cool, coat both sides with dressing and arrange attractively on platter. Spoon any remaining dressing over top. At this point, store paillards, covered, and refrigerate at least 12 hours and up to 48 hours. Bring to room temperature and sprinkle with garnishes before serving.

MAKES 6 TO 8 SERVINGS.

★HOT TRIVIA★

How did Some Like It Hot *fare at the Academy Awards?*
Although nominated for Best Director, Best Actor (Jack Lemmon),
Best Screenplay, and Best Photography (Charles Lang, Jr.),
only costume designer Orry-Kelly won an Oscar.

SUNSET TOMATO SALAD WITH "TYPE O" DRESSING

JOE: Well it was my freshman year at Princeton—there was this girl—her name was Nellie—her father was vice-president of Hupmobile—she wore glasses, too. That summer we spent our vacation at the Grand Canyon. We were standing on the highest ledge, watching the sunset—suddenly we had an impulse to kiss. I took off my glasses—she took off her glasses. I took a step toward her—she took a step toward me—

SUGAR: Oh, no!

JOE: Yes. Eight hours later they brought her up by mule. I gave her three blood transfusions—we had the same blood type—Type O—it was too late.

DRESSING

$\frac{1}{4}$ cup (60 ml) red wine vinegar

$\frac{1}{4}$ teaspoon sea salt or to taste

$\frac{1}{4}$ teaspoon sugar

freshly ground pepper and Tabasco to taste

2 cloves garlic, peeled and finely minced

1 shallot, peeled and minced

2 tablespoons fresh marjoram, finely minced (if unavailable, omit or substitute fresh parsley or basil)

12 oil-packed sundried tomatoes, minced

$\frac{3}{4}$ cup (180 ml) extra-virgin olive oil mixed with 2 tablespoons oil from sundried tomatoes

6 large ripe tomatoes, sliced crosswise $\frac{1}{4}$-inch (6.5-mm) thick

2 shallots, peeled and sliced crosswise paper thin

2 tablespoons finely minced parsley or chives

In small mixing bowl, whisk together dressing ingredients except oils. Add mixed oils in steady stream while whisking until emulsion is formed. Adjust seasoning. Arrange tomato slices attractively on platter or on 6 individual plates with sliced shallots on top. Drizzle about 2 tablespoons dressing over each individual salad or about 1 cup

(240 ml) dressing over salad if on platter. Garnish with chopped herbs. Salad can be prepared and left plated at room temperature for up to 1 hour before serving.

MAKES 6 SERVINGS.

SNAPPY SAFFRON RICE SALAD

1½ cups (240 g) long-grain white rice
5 tablespoons extra-virgin olive oil, divided
3 cloves garlic, peeled and finely minced
½ cup (60 g) finely diced onion
1 teaspoon saffron threads, crushed
2½ cups (600 ml) water
1½ teaspoons sea salt
3 teaspoons white wine vinegar or freshly squeezed lime juice
one 10-ounce (300 g) package frozen peas,
cooked according to package directions
⅓ cup (40 g) thinly sliced whole scallions
⅓ cup (26 g) finely minced fresh cilantro
salt, freshly ground pepper, and Tabasco to taste

Wash rice in several rinses of cold water until water is clear. Drain and set aside. Heat 2 tablespoons olive oil in heavy medium saucepan over low heat. Add garlic, onion, and saffron and cook until onions are translucent, about 5 minutes. Add water and salt and bring to boil over medium-high heat. Stir in rice and cook without further stirring, uncovered, until water is almost completely absorbed, about 10 minutes. Cover rice and turn heat to lowest possible setting. Cook another 10 to 15 minutes until rice is completely dry. Some rice may stick to bottom of pan. When rice has cooled to lukewarm, stir in remaining 3 tablespoons olive oil, vinegar or lime juice, and peas. When cool, add scallions and cilantro and season to taste. Salad can be refrigerated up to 24 hours, but bring to room temperature, toss in extra tablespoon of olive oil, and adjust seasoning again before serving.

MAKES 6 SERVINGS.

HOPELE/ILY PEPPERY LEMMON BI/CUIT/

SUGAR: How can you think about food at a time like this?
JOE: What else is there for me?
SUGAR: Is it that hopeless?
JOE: My family did everything they could—hired the most beautiful
French upstairs maids, got a special tutor to read me all the books that
were banned in Boston, imported a whole troupe of Balinese dancers with
bells on their ankles and those long fingernails—what a waste of money!

2 cups (240 g) cake flour
1 tablespoon baking powder
3/4 teaspoon sea salt
1 tablespoon crushed red peppercorns
(or mixed colored peppercorns or 1 1/2 teaspoons
coarsely ground black peppercorns)
3/4 to 1 cup (180 to 240 ml) heavy cream
finely grated zest of 1 large lemon
4 tablespoons melted unsalted butter

Preheat oven to 400° F (200° C). Sift cake flour, baking powder, and salt. Stir in
pepper. Stir 3/4 cup (180 ml) cream with lemon zest in electric mixer. Add dry
ingredients and mix on low speed until just combined, approximately 30 seconds or
less. Dough should be on dry side, but if too dry and not holding together, add a
little more cream. Form dough into ball. Place on floured board and with rolling
pin, roll to 1-inch (2.5-cm) thickness. Cut with 2 1/2-inch (6.5-cm) round cookie
cutter or glass. Reroll scraps until all dough has been used. Place biscuits 1 inch
(2.5 cm) apart on greased or parchment-lined baking sheet. Using kitchen brush,
paint tops of biscuits with melted butter and bake in middle of preheated oven
until light gold, 10 to 15 minutes.

MAKES 8 TO 10 BISCUITS 2 1/2 INCHES (6.5 CM) IN DIAMETER.

COCONUT BRYN MAWR
BROWNIES

JOE: I heard a very sad story about a girl who went to Bryn Mawr. She squealed on her roommate, and they found her strangled with her own brassiere.

$\frac{1}{2}$ cup (120 g) unsalted butter
2 ounces (60 g) unsweetened chocolate, chopped
$\frac{1}{4}$ teaspoon cinnamon
$\frac{1}{4}$ teaspoon instant coffee powder, preferably espresso
2 large eggs
1 cup (240 g) sugar
$\frac{1}{2}$ teaspoon vanilla extract
$\frac{1}{2}$ cup (60 g) all-purpose flour
$\frac{1}{4}$ teaspoon sea salt
$\frac{1}{2}$ teaspoon baking powder
1 cup (180 g) semisweet chocolate chips or chopped chocolate
1 cup (80 g) sweetened shredded coconut

Preheat oven to 325° F (165° C). Melt butter and unsweetened chocolate with cinnamon and coffee in top half of double boiler set over barely simmering water. Set aside and cool to lukewarm. With wire whisk or in bowl of electric mixer, beat eggs with sugar until light and fluffy, about 5 minutes. Beat in vanilla. Sift together flour, salt, and baking powder. Add dry ingredients to batter and beat until well combined. Stir in cooled chocolate mixture and then chocolate chips and coconut. Transfer batter to buttered and floured 9 × 9-inch (23 × 23-cm) baking pan, spreading evenly with knife or spatula. Place pan in middle of preheated oven. Bake 25 to 30 minutes or until done. Cool on wire rack. When cool, cut into 9 squares.

MAKES 9 LARGE BROWNIES.

BIRTHDAY BANQUET FOR SPATS

SPATS: Hello, copper. What brings you down to Florida?

MULLIGAN: I heard you opera-lovers were having a little rally, so I thought I better be around in case anybody decides to sing.

BONAPARTE'S
BLACK BEAN SOUP

BONAPARTE: Thank you, fellow opera-lovers. It's been ten years since I elected myself president of this organization—and if I say so myself, you made the right choice. Let's look at the record. We have fought off the crackpots who want to repeal Prohibition and destroy the American home—by bringing back the corner saloon. We have stamped out the fly-by-night operators who endangered public health by brewing gin in their own bathtubs, which is very unsanitary. We have made a real contribution to national prosperity—we are helping the automobile industry by buying all those trucks, the glass industry by using all those bottles, and the steel industry—you know, all those corkscrews. And what's good for the country is good for us. In the last fiscal year, our income was a hundred and twelve million dollars before taxes—only we ain't paying no taxes.

2 cups (320 g) black turtle beans
1/2 pound (230 g) smoky bacon
1 large onion, peeled and chopped
3 large cloves garlic, peeled and minced
4 carrots, peeled and chopped
4 jalapeño peppers, seeds and ribs removed, finely minced
4 ribs celery (including some leaves if possible), chopped
1 quart (1 liter) chicken or vegetable stock
2 ham hocks or 1 large meaty ham bone
1 bay leaf
1/4 cup (20 g) chopped fresh parsley
1/2 teaspoon peppercorns
2 tablespoons dark molasses
2 tablespoons orange juice concentrate
1 tablespoon Dijon mustard
1 teaspoon sea salt or more to taste
1/4 cup (60 ml) dry sherry

2 tablespoons freshly squeezed lime juice
freshly ground pepper and Tabasco to taste
sour cream or yogurt for garnish

Rinse and pick over beans. Add cold water to cover by 3 inches (7.5 cm). Soak overnight (if weather is very warm, refrigerate). Cut bacon into ¼-inch (6.5-mm) dice. Cook bacon in large soup pot over low heat, stirring occasionally until very crisp. With slotted spoon, transfer bacon to several thicknesses of paper towels and blot to remove as much grease as possible. Reserve these bacon lardons to use as garnish. Do not discard grease in pot. Add onion, garlic, carrots, jalapeños, and celery to pot. Cook over low heat until vegetables soften, 10 to 15 minutes. Add beans and their soaking liquid, stock, ham hocks, bay leaf, parsley, peppercorns, molasses, juice concentrate, and mustard to pot. Cover and simmer over very low heat for 30 minutes. Add salt and continue cooking, partially covered, until beans are very tender, 1½ to 3 hours. (Cooking time will depend on age of beans and how long they've soaked.) Add water periodically if soup becomes too thick. When beans are tender, remove ham hocks from soup. Cut meat from bones and into ½-inch (13-mm) dice. Discard bones and bay leaf. Add sherry and lime juice to soup along with diced ham. Simmer about 10 more minutes and adjust seasonings with salt, pepper, Tabasco, and possibly more lime juice. Serve soup in hot bowls garnished with sour cream or yogurt and reserved bacon lardons.

MAKES 8 SERVINGS.

★HOT TRIVIA★

Was Some Like It Hot *censored anywhere when it was first released?*
The state of Kansas decided the film contained material "regarded as too disturbing for Kansasans." The censors didn't mind the cross-dressing, but they said some of the intimate scenes between Tony Curtis and Marilyn Monroe had to go. (from *Inside Oscar*)

TOOTHPICK CHARLIE'S SPICY CRAB CAKES

1 cup (120 g) minced onion
3 cloves garlic, peeled and minced
2 jalapeño peppers, seeds and ribs removed, finely minced
4 anchovy fillets, finely minced
3/4 cup (180 ml) unflavored vegetable oil
6 tablespoons freshly squeezed lemon juice
4 egg yolks at room temperature
1/4 teaspoon Tabasco
1 tablespoon Worcestershire sauce
1/4 cup (60 g) Creole or Dijon mustard
1/2 teaspoon sea salt or to taste
2 pounds (920 g) fresh lump crab meat
1 cup (120 g) soft fresh bread crumbs
5 whole scallions, sliced very thin
1/2 cup (40 g) finely minced fresh parsley or cilantro
2 to 3 cups (240 to 360 g) dry unseasoned bread crumbs for dredging
3 to 6 tablespoons unsalted butter and 3 to 6 tablespoons vegetable oil

Set medium saucepan over low heat and cook onion, garlic, jalapeños, and anchovies with 3/4 cup (180 ml) vegetable oil, stirring frequently, until onion is translucent. While vegetables are cooking, whisk together lemon juice, egg yolks, Tabasco, Worcestershire, mustard, and salt. When vegetables are cooked, whisk them little by little into yolk mixture until emulsion forms. This mayonnaise may seem a bit thin but will thicken as it cools. Cool mayonnaise over ice and then refrigerate 1 to 2 hours. It is even better, but not necessary, to make it a day ahead and allow to thicken in refrigerator overnight.

To make crab cakes, mix cooled mayonnaise, crab meat, bread crumbs, scallions, and parsley or cilantro in medium bowl. Taste for seasoning. Crab cakes should be highly spiced. Put bread crumbs for dredging on baking sheet or large platter. Divide crab mixture into 16 balls. Working over baking sheet or platter, form each ball into patty and then dredge heavily with crumbs. Place cakes on another baking sheet or platter as they are finished. To firm crab cakes up before cooking, refrigerate at least 2 hours or overnight, covered. To cook crab cakes, preheat oven to 375° F (190° C). Melt butter with oil in large skillet (preferably nonstick) over medium heat. When pan is very hot, gently place as many crab cakes as will fit in it without crowding. Cook until golden and then turn and brown other side, about 2 minutes per side. Work in batches if skillet is not large enough to hold all cakes and add more butter and oil as needed. As cakes are browned, transfer to baking sheet. When all 16 are done, place baking sheet in oven for 5 minutes to finish cooking. Serve immediately, accompanied by Spats Colombo's Creole Mayonnaise (recipe follows).

MAKES 16 CRAB CAKES.

NOTE: Pineapple-Papaya Saxophone-Playing Salsa (p. 23) also complements crab cakes nicely.

SPATS COLOMBO'S CREOLE MAYONNAISE

½ cup (120 g) mayonnaise
½ cup (120 g) Zatarain's Creole Mustard or other grainy mustard
2 cloves garlic, peeled and finely minced
2 tablespoons finely minced chives or scallions (white and green parts)
1 teaspoon (or more to taste) finely minced serrano or
Scotch bonnet pepper, seeds and ribs removed
3 tablespoons golden raisins, finely minced
3 tablespoons finely julienned fresh mint leaves
3 tablespoons finely minced fresh parsley or cilantro
1 tablespoon frozen orange juice concentrate, defrosted
1 tablespoon freshly squeezed lime juice

Mix together all ingredients in small bowl. Allow to rest 1 hour at room temperature before serving. This will keep for up to 1 week, covered, in refrigerator.

MAKES APPROXIMATELY 1¾ CUPS (420 G).

SPATS: Spats Colombo—delegate from Chicago—South Side chapter.
PARADISE: Hi, Spats. We was laying eight to one you wouldn't show.
SPATS: Why wouldn't I?
PARADISE: We thought you was all broken up about Toothpick Charlie.
SPATS: Well, we all got to go sometime.
PARADISE: Yeah. You never know who's going to be next.

AVOCADO SALSA

1 medium tomato, finely diced
1/3 cup (40 g) finely diced peeled red onion
2 cloves garlic, peeled and minced
1/4 cup (20 g) finely minced fresh parsley or cilantro
2 tablespoons finely minced chives or scallion tops
1 jalapeño pepper, seeds and ribs removed, finely minced
(for more heat, slice paper thin and leave in seeds)
2 teaspoons ground cumin seed, toasted
1 teaspoon chili powder (or more to taste)
freshly squeezed and finely grated zest of 1 lime
2 avocados, ripe but still firm
sea salt, freshly ground pepper, and Tabasco to taste

Toss together first 9 ingredients in mixing bowl. Set aside and allow flavors to combine for at least 1 hour. When ready to serve, peel, pit, and dice avocados and toss with other ingredients. Adjust seasoning with salt, pepper, and Tabasco. Serve immediately to prevent avocado from turning brown.

MAKES APPROXIMATELY 3 CUPS (720 G).

MULLIGAN'S CORN AND BUTTERMILK SPOONBREAD

MULLIGAN: Don't worry, Spats. One of these days we'll dig up those two guys.
SPATS: That's what you'll have to do—dig `em up!

1½ (360 ml) cups water
1½ teaspoons sea salt
¼ teaspoon freshly ground black pepper
few drops Tabasco
4 tablespoons unsalted butter
¾ cup (90 g) cornmeal
2 cups (320 g) fresh corn kernels or defrosted frozen corn, divided
3 eggs, separated and at room temperature
1½ cups (360 ml) buttermilk
pinch each of sea salt and cream of tartar

Preheat oven to 425° F (215° C) and butter 9- or 10-inch (23- or 25-cm) square baking dish. In small saucepan, simmer water together with salt, pepper, Tabasco, and butter. When butter has melted, slowly add cornmeal, whisking constantly to avoid lumps. Continue to cook and whisk a minute or so until thickened. Remove pan from heat and set aside. In food processor or blender, purée 1 cup (160 g) corn kernels with egg yolks and buttermilk. Add warm cornmeal mixture and process to combine. Transfer purée to large mixing bowl and stir in remaining corn kernels. With wire whisk or electric mixer, beat egg whites with pinch salt and pinch cream of tartar until soft peaks form. Stir ¼ beaten whites into corn batter and then fold in rest. Spoon mixture into buttered baking dish and place in oven. Bake for 25 minutes or until golden and set around outside but still soft in center. Serve hot or lukewarm.

MAKES 6 SERVINGS.

CONFETTI COLESLAW

SUGAR: 414—that's the same room number I had in Cincinnati—
my last time around with a male band. What a heel he was.
JOE: Saxophone player?
SUGAR: What else? And was I ever crazy about him. Two in the
morning, he sent me down for knockwurst and potato salad—they were out
of potato salad, so I brought coleslaw—so he threw it right in my face.

DRESSING
1/4 cup (60 ml) cider or malt vinegar
1 tablespoon water
2 tablespoons mild honey or light brown sugar
1 cup (240 g) mayonnaise
1/2 cup (120 g) sour cream or yogurt
1/4 cup (60 ml) heavy cream
1 tablespoon white horseradish
2 teaspoons peeled and grated fresh ginger
4 teaspoons dry mustard
1 1/4 teaspoons sea salt or to taste
several drops Tabasco
freshly ground black pepper to taste

SLAW
1 head green cabbage (1/2 head green and 1/2 head red is even prettier)
3 carrots, peeled and coarsely grated or julienned
6 whole scallions, trimmed and cut into thin rings
1 green bell pepper, seeds and ribs removed, finely diced
1 red bell pepper, seeds and ribs removed, finely diced
1 jalapeño pepper, seeds and ribs removed, finely minced
3 tablespoons finely minced fresh parsley

To make dressing, whisk vinegar and water with honey or sugar until latter is dissolved. Add rest of dressing ingredients and whisk until combined. Adjust seasoning. Cut cabbage vertically into 4 wedges. Remove outer leaves and core. Shred cabbage quarters finely into large bowl. Add carrots, scallions, all peppers, and parsley to cabbage and toss well. Add dressing and toss again. Refrigerate for several hours or even better, overnight. Adjust seasoning before serving.

MAKES ABOUT 3 QUARTS (3 LITERS).

BANG-UP BANANA CAKE

SECOND OFFICIAL: (handing him a submachine gun) And don't mess up the cake—I promised to bring back a piece to my kids.

12 tablespoons (180 g) unsalted butter
1 cup (240 g) sugar
3 egg yolks
2 teaspoons vanilla extract
2 cups (240 g) all-purpose flour
2 teaspoons baking powder
1 teaspoon baking soda
1/4 teaspoon sea salt
1 teaspoon cinnamon
1/4 teaspoon freshly ground nutmeg
3 large or 4 small very ripe bananas (overripe is best), quartered
1/3 cup (80 ml) buttermilk
3 egg whites, at room temperature
large pinch sea salt
1/4 teaspoon cream of tartar
4 ripe to firm bananas, sliced 1/4-inch (6.5-mm) thick for filling
1 recipe Daphne's Naturally Blonde Frosting (page 62)

Preheat oven to 350° F (180° C). Generously butter and flour 9-inch (23-cm) springform pan. Cream together butter and sugar with electric mixer until light and fluffy, about 10 minutes. Add egg yolks and vanilla and beat 5 minutes more, scraping down sides of bowl with rubber spatula as necessary. Sift together flour, baking powder, baking soda, salt, cinnamon, and nutmeg and set aside. Process bananas and buttermilk in food processor until smooth, or mash bananas and whisk them with buttermilk in small bowl. Set aside. Turn mixer to lowest speed and add dry ingredients, 1/2 cup (60 g) at a time, alternating with banana mixture. Mix just until combined. Don't overbeat. With wire whisk or electric mixer, whisk egg whites with pinch of salt and cream of tartar until they hold soft peaks but are not dry. Mix 1/4 of them into batter to lighten it and then with large rubber spatula, fold batter back into remaining whites. Pour batter into prepared pan, rap once on counter to eliminate air bubbles, and place in middle of preheated oven. Bake until golden and toothpick inserted into center comes out clean, about 50 to 60 minutes. When done, cool cake 10 minutes and then remove rim of pan and place cake on wire rack to cool completely. When completely cool, invert cake and cut into 2 equal layers with large knife. Spread about 1/4 of frosting on bottom layer and cover with 1 layer of sliced bananas. Carefully put top cake layer in place and frost top and sides of cake. Serve immediately or refrigerate up to 24 hours. Remove from refrigerator 1 hour before serving.

SERVES 12 GENEROUSLY.

DAPHNE'S NATURALLY BLONDE FROSTING

20 ounces (600 g) cream cheese, at room temperature
2 cups (360 g) minus 2 tablespoons confectioners' sugar, sifted
5 teaspoons finely grated lemon zest
1 1/4 teaspoons lemon extract
pinch salt

In electric mixer or with wooden spoon, beat softened cream cheese until smooth and fluffy. Add sugar, zest, extract, and salt. Beat until combined, scraping down sides of bowl as needed. Continue to beat and scrape until mixture is light and fluffy.

OSGOOD: I called Mama—she was so happy she cried—she wants you to have her wedding gown—it's white lace.

JERRY: Osgood, I can't get married in your mother's dress. She and I—we're not built the same way.

OSGOOD: We can have it altered.

JERRY: Oh, no you don't! Look, Osgood—I'm going to level with you. We can't get married at *all*.

OSGOOD: Why not?

JERRY: Well, to begin with, I'm not a natural blonde.

OSGOOD: It doesn't matter.

JERRY: And I smoke. I smoke all the time.

OSGOOD: I don't care.

JERRY: And I have a terrible past. For three years now, I've been living with a saxophone player.

OSGOOD: I forgive you.

JERRY: And I can never have children.

OSGOOD: We'll adopt some.

JERRY: But you don't understand!
(he rips off his wig; in a male voice)
I'm a MAN!

OSGOOD: Well—nobody's perfect.

LIST OF RECIPES

COCKTAIL PARTY IN UPPER SEVEN

Greased Lightning Smoked Salmon Canapés, 6-7
Mini Grilled Cheese with Spicy Surprise Centers, 7
Buttery Chili Shortbread, 8-9
Figs in Drag, 9
Put-out Mini Pizzas, 10
Corsetless Cream Cheese Spread, 11
Chile-Marinated Chevre, 12
Fuzzy Mango Daiquiri, 13
Prohibition Piña Colada, 13
Freshly Squeezed White Rum Punch, 14
Cuba Libre, 14
Banana Republic Daiquiri, 15
Mary Lou's Mojito, 15
Joe & Jerry's Rum Runner, 16
Miami Cross-Dresser, 16-17
Honeyed Good Night Punch, 17

DINNER WITH SWEET SUE AND HER SOCIETY SYNCOPATORS

Caribbean Chicken Fricassee, 20
Bull Fiddle Fried Bananas, 21
Citrus Shrimp Salad, 22
Pineapple-Papaya Saxophone-Playing Salsa, 23
Lemmon Meringue Pie, 24
Lemmon Pie Crust, 25

BARBECUE ON THE BEACH

Sandwich of Marinated Tuna, Peppers, and Onions, 28-29
Salsa Verde, 29

Cuban Bread, 30
Shell Oil's Sliced Island Salad, 31
Shortbread Doubly Endowed with Ginger, 32
Brown Sugar Rum Ice Cream, 33

DINNER AT THE CUBAN ROADHOUSE

Succulent Crown Roast of Pork, 36
Mixed-up Mango Salsa, 37
Bienstock's Black Bean Salsa, 38
Garlic-Wilted Spinach, 39
Rich Sweet Potatoes with a Kick, 40
Curried Corn Muffins, 41
Caramelzowied Pineapple, 42
Zesty Shortcake, 43

MIDNIGHT SUPPER ON THE YACHT

New Caledonia Curried Chicken, 46-47
Sunset Tomato Salad with "Type O" Dressing, 48-49
Snappy Saffron Rice Salad, 49
Hopelessy Peppery Lemmon Biscuits, 50
Coconut Bryn Mawr Brownies, 51

BIRTHDAY BANQUET FOR SPATS

Bonaparte's Black Bean Soup, 54-55
Toothpick Charlie's Spicy Crab Cakes, 56-57
Spats Colombo's Creole Mayonnaise, 57
Avocado Salsa, 58
Mulligan's Corn and Buttermilk Spoonbread, 59
Confetti Coleslaw, 60-61
Bang-up Banana Cake, 61-62
Daphne's Naturally Blonde Frosting, 62-63

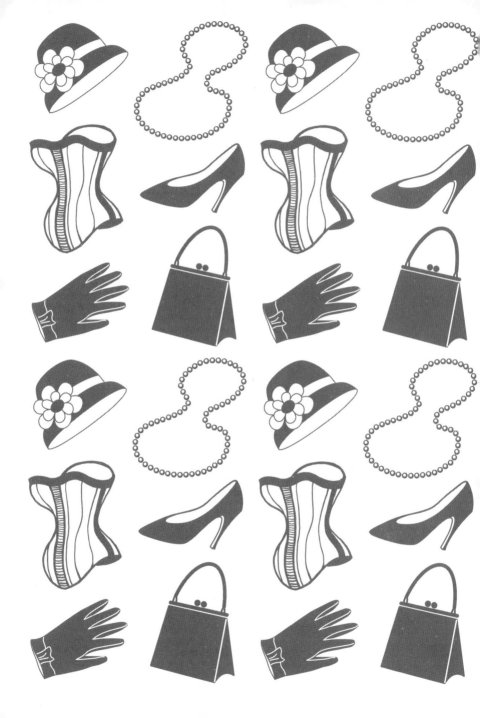